Prehistoric Animals
PREHISTORIC MAMMALS

WINDMILL
BOOKS

New York

Published in 2016 by **Windmill Books**,
an Imprint of Rosen Publishing
29 East 21st Street, New York, NY 10010

Designed and illustrated *by* David West

Cataloging-in-Publication Data
West, David.
Prehistoric mammals / by David West.
p. cm. — (Prehistoric animals)
Includes index.
ISBN 978-1-5081-9041-7 (pbk.)
ISBN 978-1-5081-9042-4 (6-pack)
ISBN 978-1-5081-9043-1 (library binding)
1. Mammals, Fossil — Juvenile literature. I. West, David, 1956-. II. Title.
QE881.W47 2016
569—d23

Manufactured in the United States of America

CPSIA Compliance Information: Batch #BW16PK: For Further Information contact Rosen Publishing, New York, New York at 1-800-237-9932

Contents

Arsinoitherium

are-sih-noy-THEE-re-um

This rhino-like mammal lived in the tropical rainforests of Northern Africa. It had two very large horns that grew side by side.

4

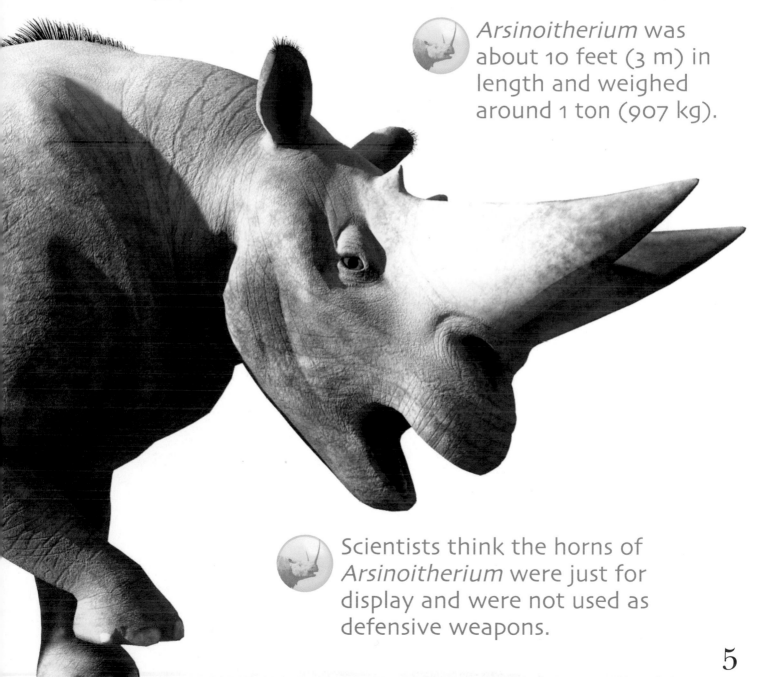

 Arsinoitherium means "Arsinoe's Beast," named after the mythical Egyptian Queen Arsinoe.

Arsinoitherium was about 10 feet (3 m) in length and weighed around 1 ton (907 kg).

Scientists think the horns of *Arsinoitherium* were just for display and were not used as defensive weapons.

Deinotherium

DIE-no-THEE-ree-um

Deinotherium was called the hoe tusker, because of its downward-facing tusks. It was a very large prehistoric relative of modern-day elephants.

Deinotherium means "Terrible Mammal."

6

Deinotherium used its downward curving tusks to strip bark from trees.

Deinotherium was about 13 feet (4 m) tall and weighed around 10 tons (9.1 metric tons).

7

Doedicurus means "Pestle Tail."

Its shell was made from around 1,800 bony plates. Each plate was 1 inch (2.5 cm) thick. Beneath this was a thick layer of fat which could absorb the blows from its rivals.

Doedicurus

DAY-dih-CORE-us

Doedicurus was a giant armadillo the size of a small family car. It lived in swampy areas and often became stuck. It had a large, spiky club at the end of its tail which it thrashed its rivals with.

Doedicurus grew up to 13 feet (4 m) in length and weighed 1.5 tons (1.4 metric tons).

Entelodon

en-TELL-oh-don

Sometimes called the "Terminator Pig," *Entelodon* was the size of a rhino. It had a vicious bite and may have hunted other animals.

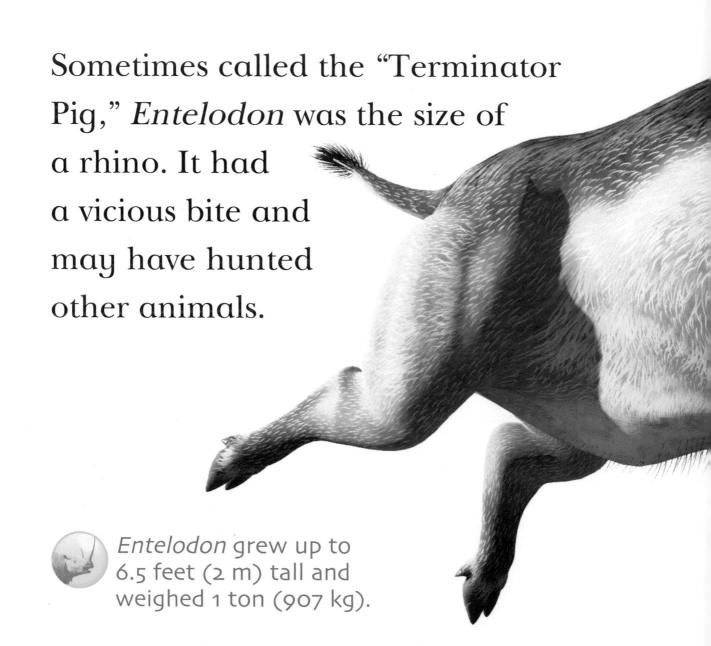

Entelodon grew up to 6.5 feet (2 m) tall and weighed 1 ton (907 kg).

Entelodon means "Perfect-toothed."

Entelodons lived in small family units. The wear on their teeth showed that they ate nuts, roots, vines, and crunched on bones.

11

Megatherium

meg-ah-THEE-re-um

Megatherium was a giant ground sloth. It ate plants using its large 2.3-foot (70 cm) claws to pull down high branches.

Megatherium grew up to 20 feet (6.1 m) in length and weighed 2–3 tons (1.8–2.7 metric tons).

Megatherium had very good defenses against predators. As well as its claws it had a coat of small, bony plates under its shaggy fur.

Megatherium means "Giant Beast."

13

Paraceratherium

PA-ra-cee-ra-THEE-re-um.

This was one of the largest land mammals that ever lived. It was eight times the size of a rhino. Its size allowed it to feed on the tallest branches where other animals couldn't reach.

 Paraceratherium grew up to 15 feet (4.5 m) tall and weighed 20 tons (18.1 metric tons).

14

Paraceratherium means "Near Horn Beast."

These animals were so big that they probably had difficulty keeping cool in the hot sun. Scientists think they may have become active at night.

15

Propalaeotherium

pro-pay-lee-oh-THEE-re-um

Propalaeotherium was an early ancestor of the horse, but it grew only to the size of a dog. Unlike modern horses it had toes, each with a small hoof on the end.

16

Propalaeotherium means "Before Old Beast."

Propalaeotherium grew up to 1–2 feet (30-60 cm) tall and weighed 22 pounds (10 kg).

Some of the fossils that have been dug up show amazing details, such as the skin and fur of these small mammals. Some even show what they last ate!

Smilodon

SMILE-oh-don

Smilodon is more commonly known as the "saber-tooth tiger." It was a powerful **predator**. Its teeth were 11 inches (28 cm) long. It used these sharp teeth to stab its victims.

Smilodon means "Saber Tooth" after the size and shape of its canine teeth.

Smilodon grew up to 6 feet (1.8 m) in length and weighed 500 pounds (227 kg).

The **La Brea Tar Pits** in California trapped hundreds of *Smilodon* in the tar, possibly as they tried to feed on mammoths already trapped there.

19

Woolly Mammoth

Mammuthus: mah-MOO-thuss

These giants lived in the cold **tundra** of the north. They had long shaggy fur to stay warm.

Mammuthus means "Earth Burrower."

The woolly mammoth was 10 feet (3 m) high and 7 tons (6.4 metric tons) in weight.

Scientists know exactly what these beasts looked like. Complete woolly mammoths have been found buried in Arctic **permafrost**.

21

The woolly rhino was hunted by early humans. We know this because there are ancient cave paintings that show this.

Coelodonta means "Hollow Tooth."

It measured up to 11 feet (3.4 m) in length, and up to 3.5 tons (3.2 metric tons) in weight.

Woolly Rhino

Coelodonta: SEE-low-DON-tah

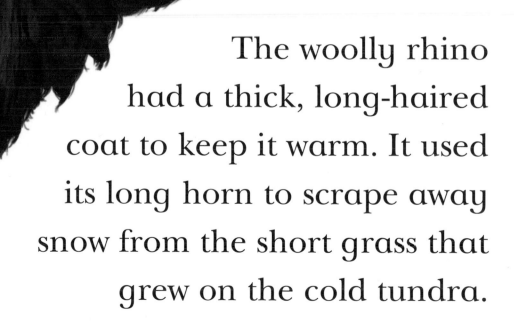

The woolly rhino had a thick, long-haired coat to keep it warm. It used its long horn to scrape away snow from the short grass that grew on the cold tundra.

23

Glossary

La Brea Tar Pits
An area in present-day California where tar seeped to the surface, trapping animals that walked into it.

permafrost
Permanently frozen soil that exists in the Arctic.

predator
An animal that hunts and kills other animals for food.

tundra
A vast Arctic region of Europe, Asia, and North America in which the subsoil is frozen.

Timeline

The prehistoric mammals in this book lived sometime during these periods, after the dinosaurs died out 65 mya.

PALEOGENE			NEOGENE		QUATERNARY	
Paleocene	Eocene	Oligocene	Miocene	Pliocene	Pleistocene	Holocene
66	56	34	23	5	2.6	0.11	0

Millions of Years Ago (mya)